A Father's Handbook

A Father's Handbook

Tim Arcand

VANTAGE PRESS
New York

FIRST EDITION

All rights reserved, including the right of
reproduction in whole or in part in any form.

Copyright © 2000 by Tim Arcand

Published by Vantage Press, Inc.
516 West 34th Street, New York, New York 10001

Manufactured in the United States of America
ISBN: 0-533-13052-2

Library of Congress Catalog Card No.: 98-91115

0 9 8 7 6 5 4 3 2 1

To Shelby, Lindsey, and Amy—thanks for the lessons
    To "Pa"—thanks for a lot of memories
And, in memory of Jerry Rustad—"The Big Guy"

Contents

Preface ix

Babies 1
Toddlers 45
Kids Will Be Kids 70

Preface

The purpose of this book is to help fathers nurture their children. In today's world, with both parents working outside of the home, and with the ever-increasing number of divorces, the role of the mother as the lone nurturer will not suffice. The role of the father must expand.

    Following is a list of practices and principles to help bring you closer to your son or daughter. These alone will not create a strong loving bond between you and your child—that will only come with a persistent, tenacious, and consistent presence in your child's life.

    These are presented as ideas and activities to help you become more involved in your child's life and to increase the amount of fun in your own. A child will laugh as often as 200 times a day, an adult laughs about twenty times a day—share their laughter and relieve some of the stress that life slings at us every day, instead of bringing that stress down on the world's most innocent people.

Enjoy being a father; it will be the greatest role of your life, for it will last for the rest of your entire life. Your children and how you raise them are your legacy.

A Father's Handbook

Babies

- Don't be afraid to hold your newborn. If she can handle being born, she can withstand a father's touch.

- Learn to change a diaper. Cloth as well as disposable diapers, you never know when you may need to improvise.

Babies

- Hug your baby every day.

- Tuck your child into bed every night when you are home.

- Know how to prepare a bottle of formula.

Babies

- Take a nap with your newborn in your lap—you'll wake up with a tremendous feeling.

- Be a part of the birth—it will be as rewarding as the conception!

- Read to your newborn child.

Babies

- Watch your baby while he sleeps. There is nothing more beautiful.

- Carry a spare <u>nuk</u> in your coat pocket.

- Display pictures of your baby in your office and replace it at least every three months, keeping the previous ones in a file.

Babies

- Take your baby to the YMCA for swimming lessons.

- Take your baby to the playground. Swing with him on your lap.

- Get a baby trailer for your bike.

Babies

- Take your baby to a petting zoo.

- Sing lullabies to your baby.

- Dance with your wife and baby in the middle of the living room.

- Taste your child's baby food.

- Give your baby her bath.

- It is okay to carry a diaper bag.

Babies

- Keep a bag in your car with a diaper, wet wipes, sunscreen, and baby-safe insect repellent.

- Don't let anyone refer to the time when you are taking care of the kids as baby-sitting.

- Kiss your baby's dirty face.

- Have a car seat in every car. You never know when it may be your turn to pick up the baby.

- Always use a car seat and place it in the rear seat.

- Make sure the child-safe door locks of your car are on.

Babies

- Introduce your baby to a litter of puppies.

- When you have had a rough day at work, look at your baby's pictures before you leave for the day. It will help to leave your problems at work and put you in a better mood.

Babies

- The first day home from the hospital can be the hardest. Make sure everything is in order before you bring your wife and baby home.

- Play a lullaby tape in your a baby's room. It will help to soothe him to sleep.

- Take a walk in the park with just yourself and your baby.

Babies

- When your baby has a cold, walk or rock him to sleep in your arms.

- On the day your baby is born, save an entire issue of the newspaper including the sales ads. It will be a treat to look back when he or she turns 18.

- Brag about your baby to your in-laws.

- Always put the toilet seat and cover down. Not only will it please your wife, but it will keep your baby out of the water.

- Resist giving your baby candy too early in life. Children will learn to hate their vegetables all too quickly.

Babies

- If you want to swing your baby—don't do it by the legs.

- Watch the maternity nurse examine your newborn. It will dispel any fears you have of holding your newborn.

Babies

- When your baby needs his shots, have him sit on your lap and hold him and comfort him immediately afterward. He will associate the pain with the doctor's office and the comfort and the diminishing of pain with his daddy.

- Accompany your wife and baby to her well-baby checks.

Babies

- Love your baby unconditionally.

- The best way to burp a baby is on your knee, supporting her head with one hand and a burp rag. This way when she spits up, it won't run down your back.

- Change your baby's first poopy diaper. After cleaning the <u>black sticky tar diaper,</u> the others will seem easy.

- Never leave your baby unattended in the bath.

- Always put a hat on your newborn, even in the summer—a baby's scalp is very sensitive to the sun.

Babies

- It is normal for babies to wear away the hair on the backs of their heads.

- Dress your baby in layers, but don't overdress him.

- Buy your baby a pair of UV protection sunglasses.

Babies

- Cheerios are a great snack for babies.

- When your baby has either the flu or diarrhea, give him Pedolyte to fight dehydration.

- When brushing your baby's teeth, use only a pea size amount of toothpaste.

Babies

- Establish a bedtime routine as early as possible and use it as long as possible. It will make bedtime easier.

- If ever you feel frustrated with your baby, put him in the crib and walk away until your frustration abates.

Babies

- Give your wife plenty of attention after the birth of your baby—post-partum blues are real.

- Newborns will cry when they are hungry, cry when they are tired, and cry when they are uncomfortable. Sometimes they will cry just because they can.

Babies

- If you cannot get your baby to fall asleep, take her for a ride in the car.

- While your wife stays home with your newborn, take your turn getting up with your baby on Friday and Saturday nights.

- A baby won't have a <u>real</u> smile until he or she is about three months. The others are gas or bowel movements.

- There is nothing greater than seeing the smile on the face of your baby when you walk into the room.

Babies

- Babies are like puppies, they will love you unconditionally.

- Baby Tylenol is a godsend during teething.

- Have the type of teething ring that can be placed in the refrigerator.

Babies

- Babies will put everything into their mouths—keep your pocket change out of the reach of your baby.

- Brush your baby's first tooth.

- Keep a baby book on the development of your baby. Eventually children will ask what their first word was, when did they get their first tooth, etc.

Babies

- When you come home with your newborn, take <u>all</u> the advice with a grain of salt and use your common sense.

- Take care when changing your newborn son's diaper. The stimulation of the cool air will promote urination.

- Learn how to swaddle your newborn—a maternity nurse will be happy to show you how.

- Remember there are a lot of things that are good for your baby that he or she will not appreciate; vaccinations, for example.

Babies

- When your child is born, open a savings account for him and save any cash gifts you receive for them.

- Never leave a baby unattended on a couch.

- Always put a baby blanket under your baby when he is lying on the floor. It is easier to wash a blanket than the carpet.

- Comb your newborn's hair with a fine comb; it will prevent cradle cap.

- Speak to your newborn when you hold and rock him. He will learn to associate your voice with comfort, security, and trust.

Babies

- Newborn babies like a set routine. Upset that routine and you could end up with an unhappy infant.

- Take a picture of your baby during his bath—it will come in handy when he starts to date.

- Take plenty of videos of your baby. As your children get older, they will love to watch themselves.

- Send video greetings from your baby to out-of-town relatives—especially grandparents.

- Keep a damp wash cloth in the refrigerator for a teething baby to chew on.

Babies

- Have the number of your pediatrician or doctor posted by the telephone.

- For a baby, the simplest things mean so much. Just smiling at your six-month-old will produce a positive response.

- Relax when you hold your newborn—if you're tense or uptight, babies can sense it. If you're relaxed, they will feel more comfortable and secure.

- When troubled, hold your newborn while he sleeps and look into his contented face—it will help to establish the priorities in your life.

Babies

- Keep your newborn protected from the wind.

- Wet wipes are convenient to use on your newborn, handy for your infant, essential with a toddler, and invaluable with preschoolers. You may be surprised that the older your children get, the more you will use.

- Give your wife a break when she needs some rest and take your newborn for a walk in the park or in the mall.

- Never bounce with your baby on your shoulders right after a feeding.

Babies

- Always remember the love and fascination you felt the first time you held your newborn. This love is unconditional. Remember it seventeen years later when your daughter puts a dent in your car.

- Don't worry about having your newborn sleep down the hall from your bedroom. You will hear her when it is feeding time.

- Be prepared for the first time your baby sleeps through the night. It <u>will</u> happen and you will wake up in a panic, come morning.

- No matter how hard you try, the first word your baby will learn is "no."

Babies

- It is normal for your newborn to lose a little of her birth weight the first few days of her life as she adjusts to eating.

- If your wife needs an extended stay in the hospital after giving birth, spend a night with her in the hospital. Many hospitals will allow you to stay on a cot in the room.

- You cannot force-feed an infant oatmeal.

- It's okay to read the sports page as well as Dr. Seuss to your infant daughter.

- Don't speed when you have your baby in the car.

Babies

- Every child is an individual—what worked with baby #1 may not work with baby #2.

- Keep a cute picture of your smiling one-year-old in your wallet. When you get angry with them at age four, seven, or ten, take out the picture and look at it before you respond.

Babies

- Remember your newborn's job is to eat, sleep, and grow.

- The only way your newborn has to communicate is through crying.

- If you are unsure about anything with the care of your baby, it is all right to call the hospital or doctor's office and ask for instructions.

Babies

- Remember, with the care of your baby, it is always better to be safe than sorry.

- When your wife and baby come home, don't forget about your wife. She may be feeling a little overwhelmed and neglected. Let her know how much you love her.

- Buy your baby a sweatshirt of your favorite team.

- Learn how to live on less sleep.

- Realize that your life has changed forever—you have now become one of the two most important people in the world to someone who won't appreciate it for twenty years!

Babies

- Take your turn packing up the diaper bag when you and your wife are going somewhere. It will give you a greater appreciation as to how much work a baby really is.

- Show off your baby to "the boys."

Toddlers

- Never dismiss your child's fears, no matter how irrational. Remember when people were afraid of the Russians? Knowledge alleviates all fears.

- You cannot reason with a two-year-old.

Toddlers

- Make as much time as you can for your children when they are little and they will make time for you when they are teenagers.

- Kiss their boo-boos away—hugs and kisses can be very healing.

Toddlers

- Never tell your child a lie—each time you're caught in a lie, you lose trust. (i.e., the shot won't hurt a bit.)

- Tell your children stories about when you were a child.

Toddlers

- When in a department store or mall, buy a helium-filled balloon and tie it to your child's wrist. This way he cannot hide amongst the clothing racks.

- Display your child's first piece of artwork in your office.

- Lie on the floor and color with your kids.

Toddlers

- Have a tea party with your daughter.

- Chase all the monsters away at night.

- Watch Saturday morning cartoons in bed with your kids.

Toddlers

- Grocery shop with your kids.

- Play trucks with your daughters.

- When your child is sick, sit by her side and rub her back or tummy.

- Play dollies with your daughter.

- Let your three-year-old daughter use one of your old T-shirts as pajamas—she'll think it's pretty neat.

- Teach your children how to dunk their cookies in milk.

Toddlers

- Let your child have your pocket change for her piggy bank.

- Turn the temperature of your water heater down to prevent scalding during bath time—it only takes a second for your baby to turn the water to hot.

- Brush your teeth with your children at the same time. You'll get a whole new perspective on oral hygiene.

- Be prepared for anything from your toddler. They can get almost anywhere in a second, even faster when your back is turned.

Toddlers

- **Teach and preach to them to stay out of the street.**

- **Child-proof your house—there is nothing more curious and cunning than a two-year-old.**

- **Use cups with sippy lids—two-year-olds enjoy spilling more than anything else.**

Toddlers

- When your toddler takes a tumble, don't over-react—this will produce an equal over-reaction from your baby.

- It's okay to have a tea party with your son.

- Climb through the tunnels at the McDonald's playroom.

Toddlers

- Administer first aid for skinned knees and elbows—remember to end with a kiss to make it all better.

- To help your child know which shoe goes to which foot, place a dot on the inseam of each shoe and teach him to match up the dots.

- Don't give your toddler bubble gum—kids don't understand the concept of not swallowing.

- Don't let your baby drink pop with caffeine—a little keeps them up all night.

- Don't give your baby chocolate—a little caffeine goes a long way.

Toddlers

- Only give your toddler suckers with safety strings instead of sticks.

- Have plenty of carpet cleaner on hand when your baby starts walking.

- Own a Radio Flyer wagon and take your children for long wagon rides.

- Let your kids decorate the Christmas tree—don't rearrange the ornaments until after they have gone to bed.

- Always give your children a penny to throw into the fountains at the malls.

Toddlers

- When your baby starts walking, remove anything they might fall on—magazine racks, knickknacks, coffee tables, etc.

- Put up baby gates on your stairways, both for going up as well as down. If your baby can climb up the stairs, she can tumble down.

- Teach your toddler to crawl down the stairs feet first.

- Boxes make the best toys for toddlers.

- Don't leave pens, pencils, or any type of writing utensil lying around for your toddler to find. Big white walls are so inviting.

Toddlers

- **Plastic pools make great sand boxes.**

- **For her first birthday, let your baby eat her own little cake with her hands, and take plenty of pictures.**

- **Know what plants in your house are poisonous and move them out of reach from your toddler.**

- Toddlers are great parrots—they will repeat everything they hear. If you don't want your eighteen-month-old using language that will raise the eyebrows of your mother-in-law, be careful of what you say.

Toddlers

- Explaining the why behind your instructions, requests, and decisions is a great concept. However your three-year-old won't understand that the family budget does not include the particular toy he desires.

- Don't expect your five-year-old to sit through an entire nine-inning baseball game.

Toddlers

- To a three-year-old, a peanut butter and jelly sandwich and potato chips are a meal.

- If your two-year-old has a nightmare, let her sleep in your bed between you and your wife.

- If you show interest in what your four-year-old says and does, he will tell you what he is doing when he is fourteen.

Toddlers

- To help your five-year-old make it through the night without wetting the bed, take him to the bathroom before you go to bed, or set your alarm clock and get up with him during the night.

- Teach your child the value of money as early as possible.

Toddlers

- You can put a stop to temper tantrums by ignoring them. Once a child learns that they don't get want they want by pitching a fit, they will end. But, if you or your wife give in just once, then you have an uphill battle.

- Be prepared for the question "why?" from your two-year old. You will hear it at least a million times—and they won't accept "because."

Toddlers

- Never send your child to bed in tears—it will be the first thing he remembers when he wakes up.

- Don't startle your son when he is getting into something he is not supposed to. His reaction could make things worse. e.g., picking up one of your wife's Precious Moment figurines and dropping it.

- Never let your toddler walk around with a glass—especially if it _is_ glass.

Kids Will Be Kids

- Never forget what it is like to be a child.

- See your children off on the first day of school every year.

- Look at the world through your child's eyes—you will be amazed how wonderful the world is.

- Use the <u>five-year-guideline:</u> if it won't matter in five years, then don't worry about it.

- Never use <u>"because I said so."</u>

- Coach your children in sports.

Kids Will Be Kids

- Jump in the pool with your kids.

- Introduce your child to kites, Slinkys, and yo-yos.

- Leave little Post-It Notes for your children to find when they get up in the morning.

- Take your daughter shopping for a dress.

- When your son or daughter wants to help daddy, be prepared for the job to take three times longer.

- Play with your kids on the playground equipment.

Kids Will Be Kids

- Jump in a pile of leaves with your kids.

- Build a snow fort for your kids.

- Learn to like <u>Chute and Ladders</u> and <u>Candyland</u>. Children love to play games, again and again.

- Learn to tolerate <u>Sesame Street</u> and <u>Barney</u>. They may be annoying, but what they teach is invaluable.

- Monitor what your children watch on TV. Remember, garbage in—garbage out.

- Walk your children to school at least once each year.

Kids Will Be Kids

- When playing games with your kids, let them win most of the time.

- Let your son watch you shave.

- A Ken doll is just a civilian with a girlfriend.

- Let your son do most of the work on his Pine Wood Derby car.

- Go to your daughter's Brownie Meeting.

- Have your kids help you make dinner for Mom.

Kids Will Be Kids

- Teach your daughters how to hold a baseball bat.

- If you want your children to be polite, say "please" and "thank you" a lot.

- When you get angry with your child, stop and take her face in your hands and look into her eyes and smile at her.

- Go on one of your child's field trips. The schools are always looking for volunteers.

- Jump rope with your kids.

- Know how to play hopscotch.

Kids Will Be Kids

- Take your child for a pony ride.

- Ride the kiddie ride with your children.

- Go on a hay ride with your children.

Kids Will Be Kids

- No matter how many toys you buy your children, they will always want more.

- Purchase the washable markers for your children.

- Meet the parents of your grade-schoolers friends.

Kids Will Be Kids

- Go to school as your child's show-and-tell.

- Take your children camping. Kids love eating every meal outside on a picnic table.

- Climb a tree with your kids.

- Take your kids to a science museum.

- Start giving your children allowances early in their lives. Give them chores to earn the allowances. It will teach them responsibility and make them feel important.

- Don't minimize your child's problems. What is important to a four-year-old or a seven-year-old is very different from what is important to an adult.

- When you daughter starts a conversation with, "Dad, promise not to laugh," don't laugh.

- Take your children to the public library.

- Avoid purchasing video games as long as possible. Buy a personal computer and stock it full of educational games. Preschoolers and grade schoolers will enjoy them as much as video games while learning at the same time.

- Children love animals. If you cannot have a pet, hang a bird feeder in your yard.

Kids Will Be Kids

- Assigning easy tasks for your young children with rewards as simple as praise and gratitude will build responsibility and self-esteem.

- Teach your children how to make paper airplanes.

- Your toddler may experience nightmares. They have not yet developed the ability to distinguish between what is real and what is <u>just a dream.</u> Monitor what they might see on television, especially right before bedtime.

- Volunteer to be your son's Cub Scout Den leader.

- **Ride your bikes through the mud puddles with your children after it has rained.**

- **Camp out in the back yard with your kids.**

- **Don't do your kids' homework for them. They won't learn anything that way. Besides, you cannot take the tests for them.**

Kids Will Be Kids

- Show your children respect and they will respect you—knock before entering their bedrooms.

- Make your yard kid-friendly. That way when you are looking for your four-year-old, you'll know where to look. Of course, your neighbors will know where to look for their four-year-olds.

- Split a popsicle with your child.

- Run through the lawn sprinkler with your kids.

- Play hopscotch on the driveway with your daughter.

- Make a playhouse out of an appliance box.

- Make a tin-can and string walkie-talkie for your children.

- Take your children to a small town parade.

- Take your children to your county or state fair. They will love to see horses, cows, and chickens.

Kids Will Be Kids

- Go wading in a pond or creek with your kids.

- Catch frogs or tadpoles with your kids.

- Remember a child's job is learn and have fun—there will be plenty of time for stress and heartache later in life.

- Have your son use his money to buy his Mother's Day gifts. He will take a little more pride in the gift he gives—even if it isn't very expensive.

- If your five-year-old daughter scores a goal in her own goal—cheer as loudly as you would if she scored a goal in the opposing goal.

- Let your kids be a part of family decisions. After letting them know what your preferences are they may surprise you and accept and agree with more decisions.

- Remember, it is never too early to talk to your kids about drugs.

- Buy your daughter a popsicle or a cone from the ice cream truck when it comes through your neighborhood.

- Plant a flower with your child. Make it his to care for and water.

- Visit a farm with your children.

Kids Will Be Kids

- When your children ask for you to do something, cut out a picture, draw an animal, etc. Take time to understand exactly what they want. It could save some frustration on your part and your child's.

- Try to answer every question to the best of your ability, in terms your four-year-old understands. The thirst for knowledge and the quest for answers are muted far too soon.

- Always have an answer for "Dad, where do babies come from?"

- Read to your children, especially as they start to learn to read. Hearing your voice inflections of a story will aid in their development of reading a story.

Kids Will Be Kids

- Don't emphasize winning with your grade-schoolers. The nature of competition and games is there will be a winner and a loser. Emphasize the <u>fun</u> in playing the game. Besides, within an hour of the game, they won't remember if they won or lost, and more importantly—won't care.

- Don't push your kids into any one sport or activity. Let them try as many as possible and decide which they enjoy.

- Make sandcastles with your kids at the beach.

- When you have to travel for business, call home every night at bedtime.

- With discipline, as in all things in life, consistency is best.

- It is okay to wrestle and roughhouse with your daughters.

- Set aside some one-on-one time every month for each of your children.

- Look at your child when you answer his questions.

- Live by the Golden Rule: Treat your children as you want them to treat you.

- Lie out in the back yard and look at the stars with your child.

Kids Will Be Kids

- **Set a good example—finish your milk and eat your vegetables.**

- **Take your child to lunch during the week.**

- **Take your children to the zoo and the circus.**

- Eat ice cream with your kids.

- Always take time to listen.

- Reflect the excitement your children present.

- Help out in your child's kindergarten class—the schools are always looking for volunteers; take advantage of the time when being seen with your dad is still <u>cool</u>.

- Don't become the disciplinarian in the family—set the ground rules with your wife. Don't ever let the phrase, <u>wait till your father gets home</u> . . . be used.

- Make pancakes and sausage on Saturday mornings.

- When you're feeling down, a hug from your child will help more than anything else.

- Lie in the grass and look at clouds with your kids.

Kids Will Be Kids

- **Never say, <u>that's stupid</u>.**

- **Take your daughter fishing.**

- **Don't smoke around your children, especially while in the car with them. Better yet, don't smoke at all.**

- Drop everything when your child excitedly shouts, "Dad, look at this!"

- Eat popcorn on the couch with your son.

- Learn how to use a needle and thread. You'll receive a hero's welcome upon the successful completion of Teddy's operation to repair a tear.

- Know how to remove splinters from little fingers and toes.

- Say <u>"I love you"</u> for no reason.

- Give each of your children a flower, and one per child to your wife.

- Send your child a card from work.

- Keep a piece of your child's artwork in your briefcase. It will brighten your day when you have to travel.

- Never discipline when you are angry.

Kids Will Be Kids

- **Never, ever spank in anger.**

- **Keep your promises—always. Don't make promises you cannot keep.**

- **Never fight with your wife in front of your children.**

- Play hide-and-seek with your kids.

- Pick wild flowers with your children.

- Plant a tree for each of your children.

Kids Will Be Kids

- A folding table with a blanket over it makes a great fort. Build one in the middle of the living room.

- Come home from work and shout, "Who wants to go out for ice cream?"

- Bring home your kids' favorite pizza for dinner.

Kids Will Be Kids

- Eat macaroni and cheese with your kids.

- Catch butterflies and fireflies with your kids.

- Don't do work at home while your kids are up.

Kids Will Be Kids

- Don't do your taxes while your children are around.

- Pray.

- Never use phrases like <u>you're bad</u>; instead refer to their behavior; "That was a <u>bad thing you did</u>."

- As with your promises, keep your threats. Make them realistic and follow through. If you have to carry a crying child out of the mall for running off or misbehaving, it will have a lasting impression on them.

Kids Will Be Kids

- Don't let the fear of embarrassment prevent you from disciplining your child in public. Some things, like not running into the street, are much more important than the stares you <u>may</u> get from people looking at your crying child.

- Read <u>How to Talk So Kids Will Listen & Listen So Kids Will Talk</u>, by Adele Faber and Elaine Mazlish.

- Grilled cheese made easy: Toast two pieces of bread in the toaster and place a piece of American cheese between the slices and melt in the microwave. Not only quick and easy, but is doesn't require any butter and is lower in fat.

- Catch your kids being good.

- Plant a garden with your children.

Kids Will Be Kids

- **Bake cookies with your kids.**

- **Teach your daughters how to change a flat tire.**

- **When you take your kids trick-or-treating, wear a costume.**

Kids Will Be Kids

- Never take away your children's dreams—don't tell them they can't do it.

- Your kids will not appreciate everything you do for them until they turn 20—at the earliest.

- Remember the best thing you can give your babies and children is yourself.

Kids Will Be Kids

- Always carve pumpkins and dye Easter eggs with your children for as long as they want.

- Never punish the act of honesty.

- Introduce your children to God and Jesus early in their lives.

- Don't let your children watch violent TV with bad language—they will learn it soon enough.

- Laugh at your children's jokes.

- Let your children know it is O.K. to make mistakes.

- Set a good example: Never use <u>"Do as I say, not as I do."</u>

- Read <u>The 7 Habits of Highly Effective Families</u>, by Stephen Covey.

- If your children participate in sports, or dance or music lessons, always attend their games or recitals.

- Always have film in your camera—you never know when one of life's firsts will occur.

- Always have a tape in the camcorder and a charged battery ready.

- Have the number of your local Poison Control Center posted by the phone.

- Things earned are better tended and cared for than things given.

- When you go for a walk, hold your wife's and your daughter's hand for as long they will let you.

- Don't limit your children's potential—tell them they can do anything they set their minds to. If they think they can—they can.

- Remember: it is true, <u>As you sow, so shall you reap</u>. Show children the right path and they will follow.

- Being a child is a full-time job. It is what they do. So is being a father; there are no days off, or holidays.

Kids Will Be Kids

- Think of yourself as your wife's tag-team partner in parenting.

- You cannot buy your children's love, admiration, or respect.

- No matter how hard you and your wife may try, there will be times of hurt feelings and misunderstandings. Letting your children know that you love them unconditionally before and after these times will help to get you through.

- Don't complain about your children's messy room if your garage is not in order.

Kids Will Be Kids

- Surprise your wife and children by taking a half-day's vacation and bringing home lunch.

- Take your kids on a picnic.

- In the winter, go sliding with your kids.

- Sleep in the living room with your kids on a Friday night.

- Breakfast cereal makes a great bedtime snack—with or without milk.

- You cannot teach your child to wake up during the night to go to the bathroom, it has to come naturally.

Kids Will Be Kids

- Make a list of the five sayings your father used that you hated to hear when you were young. Then vow never to use them.

- Make S'mores in the microwave for your kids.

- Listen, not only with your ears, but with your eyes—hear what your child is not saying. Learn your child's body language.

- Whenever your son or daughter has done something wrong, but admits to it, reward the honesty. Let them know that telling the truth is always best. It's easier to teach this to a three-year-old than a ten-year-old, or a fifteen-year-old.

Kids Will Be Kids

- Give your children options. Either an apple or a banana for a snack, whether to go to the beach or the playground? It will help them to weigh the options and make decisions, something that gets harder as life proceeds.

- Teach your children to pray. There is nothing more precious than listening to a child talk to God.

- The Spirit of a child is a fragile thing—take care when disciplining and reprimanding.

- Don't pick up after your son. <u>Help</u> him pick up.

- Don't just drop your son or daughter off at a party, practice, dance, or game. Accompany them to whoever is in charge.

Kids Will Be Kids

- When you make a mistake—admit it and apologize in front of your children. They will learn that everyone makes mistakes and how to handle them.

- Learn to laugh at yourself, especially in front of your kids. It will help them learn how to handle teasing.

- When disciplining your daughter, avoid embarrassing her in public. The resentment felt may just make things worse.

- If you don't take the time to listen to your kids, someone else will.

- Practice all the good habits you want your kids to have.

- Take every opportunity you can to teach your kids. Finding a toad in the yard can be very educational.

- There are no quick fixes or easy formulas to raising a child. The best practice is to love the child unconditionally and follow your own good common sense as well as all the guidance that God provides.

- Watch a sunset at least once a year with your wife and children.

- Carry a disposable camera in the glove compartment of your vehicle. You never know when a <u>Kodak moment</u> will occur.

Kids Will Be Kids

- When you go camping with your kids, build a campfire every night, even if it's warm. A fire can enliven a family's conversation better than television.

- Turn the TV off one night every week and have a <u>Game Night</u>. Let the kids pick the game.

- Write a Family Mission Statement. Have your kids participate in creating it.

- Take time to appreciate the <u>little moments</u> in life with your kids. When you look back, they will add up.

Kids Will Be Kids

- Praise your children when they do even the little things right—like picking up their toys, or cleaning their places at the table. It will reinforce a positive behavior.

- Always focus on the positive—tell your children what or how you want things done, not what you don't want (i.e., "<u>close the door softly</u>" instead of "<u>don't slam the door!</u>").

- Make sure you know how your children are doing in school at all times. It gives you more time to work on any needed areas and eliminates surprises in parent-teacher conferences.

- Remember kids do not have the luxury of experience—they will make a lot of mistakes. It is a part of learning and growing.

Kids Will Be Kids

- As the old saying goes . . . "<u>give me a fish and I eat for a day. Teach me to fish and I eat for a lifetime.</u>" So it is with your children. Let them do some small things for themselves. It will make them feel good about themselves, and in the long run make them more self-sufficient.

- If you are unsure what to do in certain situations, ask your father what he would do; there is no substitute for experience. Then follow your heart.

- After going sliding or building a snowman, make hot cocoa with marshmallows.

- Give each of your children his own day—a day other than his birthday. Let him pick whatever they want to do.

- Laugh with your children—as often as possible.

- Remember, fatherhood is a lifetime commitment.

- You will be your child's first teacher—take advantage of every opportunity to show and teach your child.

- Cherish every stage of your child's life. Each comes with its own treasures, whether it is the first smile, the first word, the first step, the first day of school . . .

- The time you spend with your children is more valuable than the things you buy them. Gifts can never replace the love and presence of a father.

- You can be strict without spanking or hitting.

- Remember that rules were made to be broken and there is <u>always</u> an exception to every rule. Listen to your child's explanation before reacting with punishment.

- If you listen to your children's problems intently and sincerely when they are in first grade, they will seek your advice when they are in eleventh grade.

- Just like a garden, a child requires constant tending. You reap what you sow. If you remove the weeds and provide plenty of water and sunshine, the product will be a strong plant with deep roots.

- Money and gifts are no substitute for time and communication.

- There are no shortcuts to raising good, well-mannered children.

- It's true that the acorn doesn't fall far from the tree. Your kids will be a reflection of how you raise them.

- Don't ever let <u>how it may look to others</u> keep you from doing what is right. Whether it's hugging your son in public or disciplining your daughter in front of <u>your</u> peers.

- Almost all problems result from misunderstanding of expectations. Explain exactly to your child what you want so that you both understand what is expected. It is sometimes better to <u>over-explain</u> and ensure the expected outcome is understood than to leave it implied.

- If your son gets into trouble at school, don't rush to a conclusion to one side or the other. Hear everything the teacher or principal has to say and then let your son explain his side.

- Go to as many school functions with your daughter as long as she lets you. You could end up being the chaperon at her high school Junior Prom.